The celestial hierarchy

(De Coelesti Hierarchia)

By

Pseudo-Dionysius the Areopagite

book published by
LIMOVIA.NET

TWITTER: @EBOOKLIMOVIA

isbn: 978-1489557179

Above him were seraphim, each with six wings: With two wings they covered their faces, with two they covered their feet, and with two they were flying. And they were calling to one another: "Holy, holy, holy is the LORD Almighty; the whole earth is full of his glory."

Isaiah 6:2,3

Copyright: © 2013 limovia.net - All rights reserved

the author:

Dionysius the Areopagite (Greek Διονύσιος ὁ Ἀρεοπαγίτης) was a judge of the Areopagus who, as related in the Acts of the Apostles, (Acts 17:34), was converted to Christianity by the preaching of the Apostle Paul during the Areopagus sermon. According to Dionysius of Corinth, quoted by Eusebius, this Dionysius then became the first Bishop of Athens.

In the early 6th century, a series of famous writings of a mystical nature, employing Neoplatonic language to elucidate Christian theological and mystical ideas, was ascribed to the Areopagite. They have long been recognized as pseudepigrapha and are now attributed to "Pseudo-Dionysius the Areopagite".

Dionysius was also popularly misidentified with the martyr of Gaul, Dionysius, the first Bishop of Paris, Saint Denis.

In the Eastern Orthodox Church, Dionysius the Areopagite and Saint Denis of Paris are celebrated as one commemoration on 3 October.

De Coelesti Hierarchia (Greek: Περὶ τῆς Οὐρανίας Ἱεραρχίας, On the Celestial Hierarchy) is a Pseudo-Dionysian work on angelology, written in Greek and dated to ca. the 5th century CE; it exerted great influence on scholasticism and treats at great length the hierarchies of angels.

The work has also been very influential in the development of Orthodox Christian theology.

Thomas Aquinas (Summa Theologica, I.108) follows the Hierarchia (6.7) in dividing the angels into three hierarchies each of which contains three orders, based on their proximity to God, corresponding to the nine orders of angels recognized by Pope St Gregory I.

1. Seraphim, Cherubim, and Thrones;

2. Dominations, Virtues, and Powers;

3. Principalities, Archangels, and Angels.

CHAPTER I

To my fellow-presbyter Timothy, Dionysius the Presbyter

That every divine illumination, while going forth with love in various ways to the objects of its forethought, remains one. Nor is this all: it also unifies the things illuminated.

'Every good gift and every perfect gift is from above and comes down from the Father of Lights.'[James 1:17]

Moreover, every divine procession of radiance from the Father, while constantly bounteously flowing to us, fills us anew as though with a unifying power, by recalling us to things above, and leading us to the unity of the Shepherding Father and to the Divine One. For from Him and into Him are all things, as is written in the holy Word.

Calling then upon Jesus, the Light of the Father, the Real and True, 'Which lights every man that comes into the world, by whom we have access to the Father,' the Origin of Light, let us raise our thought, according to our power, to the illumination of the most sacred doctrines handed down by the Fathers, and also as far as we may let us contemplate the Hierarchies of the Celestial Intelligences revealed to us by them in symbols for our upliftment: and admitting through the spiritual and unwavering eyes of the mind the original and super-original gift of Light of the Father who is the Source of Divinity, which shows to us images of the all-blessed Hierarchies of the Angels in figurative symbols, let us through them again strive upwards toward Its primal ray. For this Light can never be deprived of Its own intrinsic unity, and although in goodness It becomes manyness and proceeds into manifestation for the uplifting of those creatures governed by Its providence, yet It abides eternally within Itself in changeless sameness, firmly established in Its own unity, and elevates to Itself, according to their capacity, those who turn towards It, uniting them in accordance with Its own unity. For by that first divine ray we can be enlighted only insofar as It is hidden by all-various holy veils for our upliftment, and fittingly tempered to our natures by the Providence of the Father.

Wherefore that first institution of the sacred rites, judging it worthy of a supermundane copy of the Celestial Hierarchies, gave us our most holy hierarchy, and described that spiritual Hierarchy in material terms and in various compositions of forms so that we might be led, each according to his capacity, from the most holy imagery to formless, unific, elevative principles and assimilations. For the mind can by no means be directed to the spiritual presentation and contemplation of the Celestial Hierarchies unless it use the material guidance suited to it, accounting those beauties which are seen to be images of the hidden beauty, the sweet incense a symbol of spiritual dispensations, and the earthly lights a figure of the immaterial enlightenment. Similarly the details of the sacred teaching correspond to the feast of contemplation in the soul, while the ranks of order on earth reflect the Divine Concord and the disposition of the Heavenly Orders. The receiving of the most holy Eucharist symbolizes our participation of Jesus; and everything else delivered in a supermundane manner to Celestial Natures is given to us in symbols.

To further, then, the attainment of our due measure of deification, the loving Source of all mysteries, in showing to us the Celestial Hierarchies, and consecrating our hierarchy as fellowministers, according to our capacity, in the likeness of their divine ministry, depicted those supercelestial Intelligences in material images in the inspired writings of the sacred Word so that we might be guided through the sensible to the intelligible, and from sacred symbols to the

Primal Source of the Celestial Hierarchies.

CHAPTER II

That Divine and Celestial matters are fittingly revealed even through unlike symbols

I consider, then, that in the first place we must explain our conception of the purpose of each Hierarchy and the good conferred by each upon its followers; secondly we must celebrate the Celestial Hierarchies as they are revealed in the Scriptures; and finally we must say under what holy figures the descriptions in the sacred writings portray those Celestial Orders, and to what kind of purity we ought to be guided through those forms lest we, like the many, should impiously suppose that those Celestial and Divine Intelligences are many-footed or many-faced beings, or formed with the brutishness of oxen, or the savageness of lions, or the curved beaks of eagles, or the feathers of birds, or should imagine that they are some kind of fiery wheels above the heavens, or material thrones upon which the Supreme Deity may recline, or many-coloured horses, or commanders of arm- ies, or whatever else of symbolic description has been given to us in the various sacred images of the Scriptures. Theology, in its sacred utterances concerning the formless Intelligences, does indeed use poetic symbolism, having regard to our intelligence, as has been said, and providing a means of ascent fitting and natural to it by framing the sacred Scriptures in a manner designed for our upliftment.

But someone may prefer to regard the Divine Orders as pure and ineffable in their own natures, and beyond our power of vision, and may consider that the imagery of the Celestial Intelligences in the Scriptures does not really represent them, and is like a crude dramatization of the celestial names: and he may say that the theologians, in depicting wholly incorporeal natures under bodily forms should, as far as possible, make use of fitting and related images, and represent them by the most exalted, incorporeal and spiritual substances amongst ourselves, and should not endue the Celestial and Godlike Principles with a multitude of low and earthly forms. For the one would contribute in a higher degree to our ascent by dissociating incongruous images from the descriptions of Supermundane Natures, while the other impiously outrages the Divine Powers, and leads our minds into error when -we dwell upon such unholy compositions. For we might even think that the supercelestial regions are filled with herds of lions and horses, and re-echo with roaring songs of praise, and contain flocks of birds and other creatures, and the lower forms of matter, and whatever other absurd, spurious, passion-arousing and unlike forms the Scriptures use in describing their resemblances.

Nevertheless, I think that the investigation of the truth shows the most holy wisdom of the Scriptures in the representations of the Celestial Intelligences which makes the most perfect provision in each case, so that neither is dishonour done to the Divine Powers (as they may be called), nor are we bound more passionately to earth by the meanness and baseness of the images. For it might be said that the reason for attributing shapes to that which is above shape, and forms to that which is beyond form, is not only the feebleness of our intellectual power which is unable to rise at once to spiritual contemplation, and which needs to be encouraged by the natural and suitable support and upliftment which offers us forms perceptible to us of formless and supernatural contemplations, but it is also because it is most fitting that the secret doctrines, through ineffable and holy enigmas, should veil and render difficult of access for the multitude the sublime and profound truth of the supernatural Intelligences. For, as the Scripture declares, not everyone is holy, nor have all men knowledge.

Again, if anyone condemns these representations as incongruous, suggesting that it is disgraceful to fashion such base images of the divine and most holy Orders, it is sufficient to answer that the most holy Mysteries are set forth in two modes: one, by means of similar and sacred representations akin to their nature, and the other through unlike forms designed with every possible discordance and difference. For example, the mystical traditions of the enlightening Word sometimes celebrate the Sublime Blessedness of the Superessential ONE as Word, and Wisdom, and Essence; proclaiming the Intellect and Wisdom of God both essentially, as the Source of being, and also as the true Cause of existence; and they make It equivalent to Light, and call It Life.

Now although such sacred forms are more venerable, and seem in one sense to surpass the material presentation, even so they fail to express truly the Divine Likeness which verily transcends all essence and life, and which no light can fully represent; for an other word and wisdom is incomparably below It. But at other times It is extolled in a supermundane manner in the same writings, where It is named Invisible, Infinite and Unbounded, in such terms as indicate not what It is, but what It is not: for this, in my judgment, is more in accord with Its nature, since, as the Mysteries and the priestly tradition suggested, we are right in saying that It is not in the likeness of any created thing, and we cannot comprehend Its superessential, invisible and ineffable Infinity. If, therefore, the negations in the descriptions of the Divine are true, and the affirmations are inconsistent with It, the exposition of the hidden Mysteries by the use of unlike symbols accords more closely with That which is ineffable.

Accordingly this mode of description in the holy writings honours, rather than dishonours, the Holy and Celestial Orders by revealing them in unlike images, manifesting through these their supernal excellence, far beyond all mundane things. Nor, I suppose, will any reasonable man deny that discordant figures uplift the mind more than do the harmonious, for in dwelling upon the nobler images, it is probable that we might fall into the error of supposing that the Celestial Intelligences are some kind of golden beings, or shining men flashing like lightning, fair to behold, or clad in glittering apparel, raying forth harmless fire, or with such other similar forms as are assigned by theology to the Celestial Intelligences. But lest this thing befall those whose mind has conceived nothing higher than the wonders of visible beauty, the wisdom of the venerable theologists, which has power to lead us to the heights, reverently descends to the level of the inharmonious dissimilitudes, not allowing our irrational nature to remain attached to those unseemly images, but arousing the upward-turning part of the soul, and stimulating it through the ugliness of the images; since it would seem neither right nor true, even to those who cling to earthly things, that such low forms could resemble those supercelestial and divine contemplations. Moreover, it must be borne in mind that no single existing thing is entirely deprived of participation in the Beautiful, for, as the true Word says, all things are very beautiful.

Holy contemplations can therefore be derived from all things, and the above-named incongruous similitudes can be fashioned from material things to symbolize that which is intelligible and intellectual, since the intellectual has in another manner what has been attributed differently to the perceptible. For instance, passion in irrational creatures arises from the impulse of appetency, and their passion is full of all irrationality; but it is otherwise with intellectual beings in whom the energy of passion must be regarded as denoting their masculine reason and unwavering steadfastness, established in the changeless heavenly places. In the same manner, by desire in irrational creatures we mean the instinctual innate tendency towards temporal materials things, or the uncontrolled inborn appetites of mutable creatures, and the dominating irrational desires of the body which urge the whole creature towards that for which the senses crave.

But when, using unlike images, we speak of desire in connection with Intellectual Beings we must understand by this a divine love of the Immaterial, above reason and mind, and an enduring and unshakable superessential longing for pure and passionless contemplation, and true, sempiternal, intelligible participation in the most sublime and purest Light, and in the eternal and most perfect Beauty. And incontinence we must understand as that which is intense and unswerving and irresistible because of its pure and steadfast love of the Divine Beauty, and the undeviating urge towards That which most truly is to be desired.

In the case of the irrational or the insensitive things, such as brutes among living creatures, or inanimate objects, we rightly say that these are deprived of reason, or of sense-perception. But we fittingly proclaim the sovereignty, as Supermundane Beings, of the immaterial and intellectual Natures over our discursive and corporeal reasoning and sense-perceptions, which are remote from those Divine Intelligences.

It is therefore lawful to portray Celestial Beings in forms drawn from even the lowest of material things which are not discordant since they, too, having originated from That which is truly beautiful, have throughout the whole of their bodily constitution some vestiges of Intellectual Beauty, and through these we may be led to immaterial Archetypes; the similitudes being taken, as has been said, dissimilarly, and the same things being defined, not in the same way, but harmoniously and fittingly, in the case both of intellectual and sensible natures.

We shall see that the theologians mystically employ symbolical explanations not only in the case of the Celestial Orders, but even for the presentation of the Deific Principles themselves. And sometimes they celebrate Deity Itself with lofty symbolism as the Sun of justice, as the Morning Star rising mystically in the mind, or as Light shining forth unclouded and intelligibly; and sometimes they use images of things on earth, such as fire flashing forth with harmless flame, or water affording abundance of life symbolically flowing into a belly and gushing out in perpetually overflowing rivers and streams.

The lowest images are also used, such as fragrant ointment, or the corner-stone, and they even give It the forms of wild animals and liken It to the lion and panther, or name It a leopard, or a raging bear bereaved of its young. I will add, furthermore, that which appears most base and unseemly of all, namely that some renowned theologians have represented It as assuming the form of a worm. Thus all those who are wise in divine matters, and are interpreters of the mystical revelations, set apart in purity the Holy of Holies from the uninitiated and unpurified, and prefer incongruous symbols for holy things, so that divine things may not be easily accessible to the unworthy, nor may those who earnestly contemplate the divine symbols dwell upon the forms themselves as the final truth. Therefore we may celebrate the Divine Natures through the truest negations and also by the images of the lowest things in contrast with their own Likeness.

Hence there is no absurdity in portraying the Celestial Natures, for the reasons mentioned, by discordant and diverse symbols: for possibly we ourselves might not have begun to search into the Mysteries which lead us to the Heights through the careful examinations of the holy Word, had not the ugliness of the imagery of the Angels startled us, not suffering our mind to dwell upon the discordant figures, but stimulating it to leave behind all material attachments, and training it by means of that which is apparent to aspire devoutly to the supermundane ascent.

Let these things suffice touching the corporeal

and inharmonious forms used for the delineation of Angels in the sacred Scriptures. We must proceed to the definition of our conception of the Hierarchy itself, and of the blessings which are enjoyed by those who participate in it. But let our leader in the discourse be my Christ (if thus I dare name Him) who inspires all hierarchical revelation. And do thou, my son, listen, according to the law of our hierarchical tradition, with meet reverence to that which is reverently set forth, becoming through instruction inspired by the revelations; and, treasuring deep in the soul the holy Mysteries, preserve them in their unity from the unpurified multitude: for, as the Scriptures declare, it is not fitting to cast before swine that pure and beautifying and clear-shining glory of the intelligible pearls.

CHAPTER III

What is Hierarchy, and what the use of Hierarchy?

Hierarchy is, in my opinion, a holy order and knowledge and activity which, so far as is attainable, participates in the Divine Likeness, and is lifted up to the illuminations given it from God, and correspondingly towards the imitation of God.

Now the Beauty of God, being unific, good, and the Source of all perfection, is wholly free from dissimilarity, and bestows its own Light upon each according to his merit;* and in the most divine Mysteries perfects them in accordance with the unchangeable fashioning of those who are being perfected harmoniously to Itself.

The aim of Hierarchy is the greatest possible assimilation to and union with God, and by taking Him as leader in all holy wisdom, to become like Him, so far as is permitted, by contemplating intently His most Divine Beauty. Also it moulds and perfects its participants in the holy image of God like bright and spotless mirrors which receive the Ray of the Supreme Deity -which is the Source of Light; and being mystically filled with the Gift of Light, it pours it forth again abundantly, according to the Divine Law, upon those below itself. For it is not lawful for those who impart or participate in the holy Mysteries to overpass the bounds of its sacred laws; nor must they deviate from them if they seek to behold, as far as is allowed, that Deific Splendour and to be transformed into the likeness of those Divine Intelligences.

Therefore he who speaks of Hierarchy implies a certain perfectly holy Order in the likeness of the First Divine Beauty, ministering the sacred mystery of its own illuminations in hierarchical order and wisdom, being in due measure conformed to its own Principle. (1)

For each of those who is allotted a place in the Divine Order finds his perfection in being uplifted, according to his capacity , towards the Divine Likeness; and what is still more divine, he becomes, as the Scriptures say, a fellow-worker with God, and shows forth the Divine Activity revealed as far as possible 'in himself. For the holy constitution of the Hierarchy ordains that some are purified, others purify; some are enlightened, others enlighten; some are perfected, others make perfect; for in this way the divine imitation will fit each one.

Inasmuch as the Divine Bliss (to speak in human terms) is exempt from all dissimilarity, and is full of Eternal Light, perfect, in need of no perfection, purifying, illuminating, perfecting being rather Himself the holy Purification, Illumination and Perfection, above purification, above light. supremely perfect, Himself the origin of perfection and the cause of every Hierarchy, He transcends in excellence all holiness.(2)

I hold, therefore, that those who are being purified ought to be wholly perfected and free from all taint of unlikeness; those who are illuminated should be filled full with Divine Light, ascending, to the contemplative state and power with the most pure eyes of the mind; those who are being initiated, holding themselves apart from all imperfection, should become participators in the Divine Wisdom which they have contemplated.

Further it is meet that those who purify should bestow upon others from their abundance of purity their own holiness: those who illuminate, as possessing more luminous intelligence, duly receiving and again shedding forth the light, and joyously filled with holy brightness, should impart their own overflowing light to those worthy of it; finally, those who make perfect, being skilled in the mystical participations, should lead to that consummation those who are perfected by the most holy initiation of the knowledge of holy things which they have contemplated. Thus each order in the hierarchical succession is guided to the divine co-operation, and brings into manifestation, through the Grace and Power of God, that which is naturally and supernaturally in the Godhead, and which is consummated by Him superessentially, but is hierarchically manifested for man's imitation as far as is attainable, of the God-loving Celestial Intelligences.

CHAPTER IV

The meaning of the name 'Angels'.

Since, in my opinion, the nature of a hierarchy has been adequately defined, we must proceed to render honour to the Angelic Hierarchy, intently gazing with supermundane sight upon the holy imagery of it in the Scriptures, that we may be uplifted in the highest degree to their divine purity through that mystical representation, and may praise the Origin of all hierarchical knowledge with a veneration worthy of the things of God, and with devout thanksgiving.

In the first place this truth must be declared, that the superessential Deity, having through His Goodness established the essential subsistence of all, brought all things into being. For 'it is the very nature of that God which is the Supreme Cause of all to call all things to participation in Itself in proportion to the capacity and nature of each.

Wherefore all things share in that Providence which streams forth from the superessential Deific Source of all; for they would not be unless they had come into existence through participation in the Essential Principle of all things.

All inanimate things participate in It through their being; for the 'to be' of all things is the Divinity above Being Itself, the true Life. Living things participate in Its life-giving Power above all life; rational things participate in Its self-perfect and pre-eminently perfect Wisdom above all reason and intellect.

It is manifest, therefore, that those Natures which are around the Godhead have participated of It in manifold ways. On this account the holy ranks of the Celestial Beings are present with and participate in the Divine Principle in a degree far surpassing all those things which merely exist, and irrational living creatures, and rational human beings. For moulding themselves intelligibly to the imitation of God, and looking in a supermundane way to the Likeness of the Supreme Deity, and longing to form the intellectual appearance of It, they naturally have more abundant communion with Him, and with unremitting activity they tend eternally up the steep, as far as is permitted, through the ardour of their unwearying divine love, and they receive the Primal Radiance in a pure and immaterial manner, adapting themselves to this in a life wholly intellectual.

Such, therefore, are they who participate first, and in an all-various manner, in Deity, and reveal first, and in many ways, the Divine Mysteries. Wherefore they, above all, are pre-eminently worthy of the name Angel because they first receive the Divine Light, and through them are transmitted to us the revelations which are above us.

It is thus that the Law (as it is written in the Scriptures) was given to us by Angels and, both before and after the days of the Law, Angels guided our illustrious forefathers to God, either by declaring to them what they should do and leading them from error and an evil life to the straight path of truth, or by making known to them the Divine Law, or in the manner of interpreters, by showing to them holy Hierarchies, or secret visions of supermundane Mysteries, or certain divine prophecies.

Now, if anyone should say that God has shown Himself without intermediary to certain holy men, let him know beyond doubt, from the most holy Scriptures, that no man has ever seen, nor shall see, the hidden Being of God; but God has shown Himself, according to revelations which are fitting to God, to His faithful servants in holy visions adapted to the nature of the seer.

The divine theology, in the fullness of its wisdom, very rightly applies the name theophany to that beholding of God which shows the Divine Likeness, figured in Itself as a likeness in form of

That which is formless, through the uplifting of those who contemplate to the Divine; inasmuch as a Divine Light is shed upon the seers through it, and they are initiated into some participation of divine things.

By such divine visions our venerable forefathers were instructed through the mediation of the Celestial Powers. Is it not told in the holy Scriptures that the sacred Law was given to Moses by God Himself in order to teach us that in it is mirrored the divine and holy Law? Furthermore, theology wisely teaches that it was communicated to us by Angels, as though the authority of the Divine Law decreed that the second should be guided to the Divine Majesty by the first. For not solely in the case of higher and lower natures, but also for co-ordinate natures, this Law has been established by its superessential original Author: that within each Hierarchy there are first, middle and last ranks and powers, and that the higher are initiators and guides of the lower to the divine approach and illumination and union.(3)

I see that the Angels, too, were first initiated into the divine Mystery, of Jesus in His love for man, and through them the gift of that knowledge was bestowed upon us: for the divine Gabriel announced to Zachariah the high-priest that the son who should to born to him through Divine

Grace, when he was bereft of hope, would be a prophet of that Jesus who would manifest the union of the human and divine natures through the ordinance of the Good Law for the salvation of the world; and he revealed to Mary how of her should be born the Divine Mystery of the ineffable Incarnation of God.

Another Angel taught Joseph that the divine promise made to his forefather David should be perfectly fulfilled. Another brought to the shepherds the glad tidings, as to those purified by quiet withdrawal from the many, and with him a multitude of the heavenly host gave forth to all the dwellers upon earth our often-sung hymn of adoring praise.

Let us now mount upward to that most sublime of all Lights celebrated in the Scriptures: for I perceive that Jesus Himself who is the superessential Head of the supercelestial Beings above Nature, when taking our nature while still keeping His own immutable Divinity, did not turn away from the human order which He arranged and chose, but rather submitted Himself obediently to the commands given by God the Father through Angels, by whose ministrations the Father's decree touching the flight of His Son into Egypt and the return from Egypt into Judaea. was announced to Joseph. Moreover, through Angels we see Him subjecting Himself to the Father's will; for I will not recall to one who knows our sacred tradition the Angel who fortified Jesus, or even that Jesus Himself, because He came for the good work of our salvation to fulfil the law in its spiritual application, was called Angel of Good Counsel. For He Himself says, in the manner of a herald, that whatsoever He heard from the Father He announced unto us.

CHAPTER V

Why all the Celestial Beings in common are called Angels.

This, so far as we understand it, is the reason for the name Angel in the Scriptures. Now I think we should investigate the reason why theologians give the general name Angels to all the Celestial Beings, but when explaining the characteristics of the supermundane Orders they specifically give the name Angel to those who complete and conclude the Divine Celestial Hierarchies. Above these they place the choirs of Archangels, Principalities, Powers, Virtues, and those other beings who are acknowledged by the traditional scriptural teachings to be of higher rank.

Now we maintain that in these Hierarchies the higher Orders possess the illuminations and powers of the lower ranks, but the lower do not participate equally with those above them. Hence the theologians call the higher of these spiritual Orders Angels because they, too, show forth the Divine Radiance; but we can find no reason for calling the lowest choirs of the Celestial Intelligences Principalities or Thrones or Seraphim, for they do not manifest in the same degree that supremely excellent power;

but just as they guide our inspired hierarchs to the Divine Brightness known to them, so do those most holy Powers which are above them lead to the Divine Majesty those ranks which complete the Angelic Hierarchies.(4)

And this also may be added, that all can rightly be called Angels in respect of their participation in the Divine Likeness and Illumination both in the higher and lower ranks.

But now let us proceed further into detail, and with singleness of mind examine the particular sacred characteristics of each of the Celestial Orders which are set forth for us in the Scriptures.

CHAPTER VI

Which is the first Order of the Celestial Beings, which the middle, and which the last?

I hold that none but the Divine Creator by whom they were ordained is able to know fully the number and the nature of the supermundane Beings and the regulation of their sacred Hierarchies; and furthermore, that they know their own powers and illuminations and their own holy supermundane ordination. For we could not have known the mystery of these supercelestial Intelligences and all the holiness of their perfection had it not been taught to us by God through His Ministers who truly know their own natures.

Therefore we will say nothing as from ourselves, but being instructed will set forth, according to our ability, those angelic visions which the venerable theologians have beheld.

Theology has given to the Celestial Beings nine interpretative names, and among these our divine initiator distinguishes three threefold Orders.(5) In the first rank of all he places those who, as we are told, dwell eternally in the constant presence of God, and cleave to Him, and above all others are immediately united to

Him. And he says that the teachings of the holy Word testify that the most holy Thrones and many-eyed and many-winged ones, named in the Hebrew tongue Cherubim and Seraphim, are established immediately about God and nearest to Him above all others. Our venerable hierarch describes this threefold Order as a co-equal unity, and truly the most exalted of the Hierarchies, the most fully Godlike, and the most closely and immediately united to the First Light of the Godhead.

The second, he says, contains the Powers, Virtues and Dominions, and the last and lowest choirs of the Celestial Intelligences are called Angels, Archangels and Principalities.

CHAPTER VII

Of the Seraphim, Cherubim and Thrones, and their first Hierarchy.

In accepting this order of the holy Hierarchies we affirm that the names of each of the Celestial Choirs expresses its own Godlike characteristic. We are told by Hebrew scholars that the holy name Seraphim means 'those who kindle or make hot', and Cherubim denotes abundance of knowledge or an outflowing of wisdom.* Reasonably, therefore, is this first Celestial Hierarchy administered by the most transcendent Natures, since it occupies a more exalted place than all the others, being imrnediately present with God; and because of its nearness, to it are brought the first revelations and perfections of God before the rest. Therefore they are named 'The Glowing Ones', 'Streams of Wisdom', 'Thrones', in illustration of their Divine Nature.

The name Seraphim clearly indicates their ceaseless and eternal revolution about Divine Principles, their heat and keenness, the exuberance of their intense, perpetual, tireless activity, and their elevative and energetic assimilation of those below, kindling them and firing them to their own heat, and wholly purifying them by a burning and all-consuming flame; and by the unhidden, unquenchable, changeless, radiant and enlightening power, dispelling and destroying the shadows of darkness.

The name Cherubim denotes their power of knowing and beholding God, their receptivity to the highest Gift of Light, their contemplation of the Beauty of the Godhead in Its First Manifestation, and that they are filled by participation in Divine Wisdom, and bounteously outpour to those below them from their own fount of wisdom.

The name of the most glorious and exalted Thrones denotes that which is exempt from and untainted by any base and earthly thing, and the supermundane ascent up the steep. For these have no part in that which is lowest, but dwell in fullest power, immovably and perfectly established in the Most High, and receive the Divine Immanence above all passion and matter, and manifest God, being attentively open to divine participations.

This, then, is the meaning of their names, so far as we understand it: but now we must set forth our conception of the nature of this Hierarchy, for the object of every Hierarchy, as I think we have already sufficiently shown, is a steadfast devotion to the divine assimilation in the

Likeness of God; and the whole work of a Hierarchy is in the participation and the imparting of a most holy Purification, Divine Light and perfecting Knowledge.

And now I pray that I may speak worthily of those most exalted Intelligences, and as their Hierarchy is revealed in the Scriptures. It is clear that the Hierarchy is similar in its nature and has close affinity with those First Beings who are established after the Godhead, which is the Source of their Being, as though within Its Portals, transcending all - created powers, both visible and invisible. Therefore we must recognize that they are pure, not as having been cleansed from stains and defilements, nor as not admitting material images, but as far higher than all baseness, and surpassing all that is holy. As befits the highest purity, they are established above the most Godlike Powers and eternally keep their own self-motive and self-same order through the Eternal Love of God, never weakening in power, abiding most purely in their own Godlike identity, ever unshaken and unchanging. Again, they are contemplative, not as beholding intellectual or sensible symbols, nor as being uplifted to the Divine by the all-various contemplations set forth in the Scriptures, but as filled with Light higher than all immaterial knowledge, and rapt, as is meet, in the contemplation of that Beauty which is the superessential triune Origin and Creator of all beauty. In like manner they are thought worthy of fellowship with Jesus, not through sacred images which shadow forth the Divine Likeness, but as truly being close to Him in that first participation of the knowledge of His Deifying Illuminations. Moreover, the imitation of God is granted to them in a preeminent degree, and as far as their nature permits they share the divine and human virtues in primary power.

In the same manner they are perfect, not as though enlightened by an analytical knowledge of holy variety, but because they are wholly perfected through the highest and most perfect deification, possessing the highest knowledge that Angels can have of the works of God; being Hierarchs not through other holy beings, but from God Himself, and since they are uplifted to God directly by their pre-eminent power and rank, they are both established immovably beside the All-Holy, and are borne up, as far as is allowable, to the contemplation of His Intelligible and Spiritual Beauty. Being placed nearest to God, they are instructed in the true understanding of the divine works, and receive their hierarchical order in the highest degree from Deity Itself, the First Principle of Perfection.

The theologians therefore clearly show that the

lower ranks of the Celestial Beings receive the understanding of the divine works from those above them in a fitting manner, and that the highest are correspondingly enlightened in the Divine Mysteries by the Most High God Himself. (6) For some of them are shown to us as enlightened in holy matters by those above them, and we learn that He who in human form ascended to heaven is Lord of the Celestial Powers and King of Glory. And Angels are represented as questioning Him and desiring knowledge of His divine redemptive work for us, and Jesus Himself is depicted as teaching them and revealing directly to them His great goodness towards mankind. 'For I, He says, 'speak righteousness and the judgment of salvation.' Moreover, I am astonished that even the first rank of Celestial Beings, so far surpassing all the others, should reverently desire to receive the divine enlightenment in an intermediate manner. For they do not ask directly, 'Wherefore are Thy garments red?' but first eagerly question one another, showing that they seek and long for the knowledge of His divine words, without expectation of the enlightenment divinely granted them.

The first Hierarchy of the Celestial Intelligences, therefore, is purified and enlightened; being ordained by that First Perfecting Cause, uplifted directly to Himself, and filled, analogously, with the most holy purification of the boundless Light of the Supreme Perfection, untouched by any inferiority, full of Primal Light, and perfected by its union with the first-given Understanding and Knowledge.

But to sum up, I may say, not unreasonably, that the participation in Divine Knowledge is a purification, an illumination and a perfection. For it purifies from ignorance by the knowledge of the perfect Mysteries granted in due measure; it illuminates through the Divine Knowledge Itself by which it purifies the mind which formerly did not behold that which is now shown to it by the higher illumination; and it perfects by the self-same light through the abiding knowledge of the most luminous initiations.

This, so far as I know, is the first Order of Celestial Beings which are established about God, immediately encircling Him: and in perpetual purity they encompass His eternal Knowledge in that most high and eternal angelic dance, rapt in the bliss of manifold blessed contemplations, and irradiated with pure and primal splendours.

The are filled with divine food which is manifold, through the first-given outpouring, yet one through the unvaried and unific oneness of the divine banquet; and they are deemed worthy of communion and co-operation with God by reason of their assimilation to Him, as far as is possible for them, in the excellence of their natures and energies. For they know preeminently many divine matters, and they participate as far as they may in Divine Understanding and Knowledge.

Wherefore theology has given those on earth its hymns orpraise in which is divinely shown forth the great excellence of its sublime illumination. For some of that choir (to use material terms) cry out as with a voice like the sound of many waters, 'Blessed is the Glory of the Lord from His Place'; others cry aloud that most renowned and sacred hymn of highest praise to God, 'Holy, holy, holy, Lord God of Sabaoth, the whole earth is full of Thy Glory!'

Now we have already expounded to the best of our ability in the treatise on Divine Hymns these most sublime hymns of the supercelestial Intelligences, and have sufficiently dealt with them there. For the present purpose it is enough to o recall that this first Order, having been duly enlightened by the Divine Goodness in the knowledge of theology, gave to those below it, as befits angelic goodness, this teaching (to state it briefly-) that it is meet that the most august Deity, above praise, and all-praised, worthy of the highest praise, should be known and proclaimed, as far as is attainable, by the God-filled Intelligences (for, as the Scriptures say, being in the Likeness of God, the\are divine habitations of the Divine Stillness); and again, the teaching that He is a monad and tri-subsistent unity, providentially pervading all things through His Goodness, from the supercelestial Natures down to the lowest things of the earth; for He is the super-original Principle and Cause of every essence, and holds the whole universe superessentially in His irresistible embrace.

CHAPTER VIII

Of the Dominions, Virtues and Powers, and their middle Hierarchy.

Now we must pass on to the middle Order of the Celestial Intelligences, contemplating with supermundane sight, as far as we may, the Dominions and the truly majestic splendour of the Divine Virtues and Powers. For the names of these supernal Beings denote the divine characteristics of their likeness to God.

The name given to the holy Dominions signifies, I think, a certain unbounded elevation to that which is above, freedom from all that is of the earth, and from all inward inclination to the bondage of discord, a liberal superiority to harsh tyranny, an exemptness from degrading servility and from all that is low: for they are untouched by any inconsistency. They are true Lords, perpetually aspiring to true lordship, and to the Source of lordship, and they providentially fashion themselves and those below them, as far as possible, into the likeness of true lordship. They do not turn towards vain shadows, but wholly give themselves to that true Authority, forever one with the Godlike Source of lordship.

The name of the holy Virtues signifies a certain

powerful and unshakable virility welling forth into all their Godlike energies; not being weak and feeble for any reception of the divine Illuminations granted to it; mounting upwards in fullness of power to an assimilation with God; never falling away from the Divine Life through its own weakness, but ascending unwaveringly to the superessential Virtue which is the Source of virtue: fashioning itself, as far as it may, in virtue; perfectly turned towards the Source of virtue, and flowing forth providentially to those below it, abundantly filling them with virtue.

The name of the holy Powers, co-equal with the Divine Dominions and Virtues, signifies an orderly and unconfined order in the divine receptions, and the regulation of intellectual and supermundane power which never debases its authority by tyrannical force, but is irresistibly urged onward in due order to the Divine. It beneficently leads those below it, as far as possible, to the Supreme Power which is the Source of Power, which it manifests after the manner of Angels in the wellordered ranks of its own authoritative power.

This middle rank of the Celestial Intelligences, having these Godlike characteristics, is purified, illuminated and perfected in the manner already described, by the divine Illuminations bestowed upon it in a secondary manner through the first hierarchical Order, and shown forth in a secondary manifestation by the middle choir.

The knowledge which is said to be imparted by one Angel to another may be interpreted as a symbol of that perfecting which is effected from afar and made obscure because of its passage to the second rank. For, as those say who are wise in the sacred Mysteries, the direct revelations of the Divine Light impart a greater perfection than those bestowed through an intermediary; and in the same way I consider that the Order of Angels which is established nearest to the Godhead participates directly in a more resplendent light than is imparted to those who are perfected through others.

For this reason the First Intelligences are called in our priestly tradition perfective, illuminative and purificatory powers in regard to the lower Orders which are uplifted by them to the superessential Principle of all, and as far as is right for them are made partakers of the mystical purifications, illuminations and perfections. For this universal ordinance is divinely established, that the Divine Light is imparted to secondary natures through primary natures.

You will find this variously set forth by theologians, for when the Divine and Fatherly Love for man reproved the Israelites and chastened them for their salvation by delivering them for their correction into the hands of cruel and barbaric nations, and with providential guidance led them back by many paths to a better condition, and mercifully recalled them from captivity to freedom and their former happy state, one of the theologians, named Zachariah, sees one of those Angels which, as I believe are first and nearest to God (for the name Angel, as I have said, is common to all), receiving from God Himself the words of comfort, as they are called, and another Angel of lower rank going to meet the first as if to receive and partake of the light, and then receiving from him, as from a hierarch, the divine purpose, being directed to reveal to the theologian that Jerusalem should be inhabited by a great and fruitful nation.

Another theologian, Ezekiel, says that the most sacred edict came forth from the supremely glorious Godhead Itself, exalted above the Cherubim. For after the Father, as has been said, had in His mercy led the Children of Israel through disciplines to a better condition He decreed in His divine justice that the guilty should be separated from the innocent. This is first revealed to one below the Cherubim, who was girt about the loins with a sapphire, and was robed in a garment reaching to the feet, the symbol of an hierarch. But the Divine Law ordained that the other Angels armed with battle-axes should be instructed by the former respecting the divine judgment in this matter. For He directed the one to go through the midst of Jerusalem and to set a mark upon the foreheads of the innocent; but to the other Angels He said, 'Go into the city, following him, and strike, and turn not aside your eyes; but draw not near unto those upon whom is the mark'.

What could be said concerning the Angel who said to Daniel, 'The Word has gone forth'? or concerning that highest one who took the fire from the midst of the Cherubim? Or what could establish more clearly the distinction between the angelic ranks than this, that the Cherub cast the fire into the hands of him who was clothed with the sacred vestment? Or that He who called the most divine Gabriel to Himself said, 'Make this man understand the vision'? And many other similar things are related by the venerable theologians regarding the Divine Order of the Celestial Hierarchies.

By moulding itself after their likeness our own hierarchy will, as far as possible, be assimilated to it and will, in very deed, show forth, as in images, the angelic beauty; receiving its form from them, and being uplifted by them to the superessential Source of every Hierarchy.

CHAPTER IX

Of the Principalities, Archangels and Angels, and of their last Hierarchy,.

There remains for us the reverent contemplation of that sacred Order which completes the Angelic Hierarchies, and is composed of the Divine Principalities, Archangels and Angels. And first, I think, I ought to explain to the best of my ability the meanings of their holy names.

The name of the Celestial Principalities signifies their Godlike princeliness and authoritativeness in an Order which is holy and most fitting to the princely Powers, and that they are wholly turned towards the Prince of Princes, and lead others in princely fashion, and that they are formed, as far as possible, in the likeness of the Source of Principality, and reveal Its superessential order by the good Order of the princely Powers.

The choir of the holy Archangels is placed in the same threefold Order as the Celestial Principalities; for, as has been said, there is one Hierarchy and Order which includes these and the Angels. But since each Hierarchy has first, middle and last ranks, the holy Order of Archangels, through its middle position, participates in the two extremes, being joined with the most .holy Principalities and with the holy Angels.

It is joined with the Princedoms because it is turned in a princely way to the superessential Principality and, as far as it can attain, moulds itself in His likeness, and it is seen to be the cause of the union of the Angels with its own orderly and invisible leadership. It is joined with the Angels because it belongs to the interpreting Order, receiving in its turn the illuminations from the First Powers, and beneficently announcing these revelations to the Angels; and by means of the Angels it shows them forth to us in the measure of the mystical receptivity of each one who is inspired by the divine Illumination. For the Angels, as we have said, fill up and complete the lowest choir of all the Hierarchies of the Celestial Intelligences since they are the last of the Celestial Beings possessing the angelic nature. And they, indeed, are more properly named Angels by us than are those of a higher rank because their choir is more directly in contact With manifested and mundane things.

The highest Order, as we have said, being in the foremost place near the Hidden One, must be regarded as hierarchically ordering in a bidden manner the second Order; and the second Order of Dominions, Virtues and Powers, leads the Principalities, Archangels and Angels more manifestly, indeed, than the first Hierarchy, but in a more hidden manner than the Order below it; and the revealing Order of the Principalities, Archangels and Angels presides one through the other over the human hierarchies so that their elevation and turning to God and their communion and union with Him may be in order; and moreover, that the procession from God, beneficently granted to all the Hierarchies, and visiting them all in common, may be with the most holy order.

Accordingly the Word of God has given our hierarchy into the care of Angels, for Michael is called Lord of the people of Judah, and other Angels are assigned to other peoples. For the Most High established the boundaries of the nations according to the number of the Angels of God.

If someone should ask why the Hebrews alone were guided to the divine Illuminations, we should answer that the turning away of the nations to false gods ought not to be attributed to the direct guidance of Angels, but to their own refusal of the true path which leads to God, and the falling away through selflove and perversity, and similarly, the worship of things which they regarded as divine.

Even the Hebrews are said to have acted thus, for he says, 'Thou hast cast away the knowledge of God and hast gone after thine own heart'. For our life is not ruled by necessity, nor are the divine irradiations of Providential Light obscured because of the freewill of those under Its care; but it is the dissimilarity of the mental eyes which causes the Light streaming forth resplendently from the Goodness of the Father to be either totally unshared and unaccepted through their resistance to It, or causes an unequal participation, small or great, dark or bright, of that Fontal Ray which nevertheless is one and unmixed, eternally changeless, and for ever abundantly shed forth. For even if certain Gods not alien to them presided over the other nations (from which we ourselves have come forth into that illimitable and abundant sea of Divine Light which is outspread freely for all to share), yet there is one Ruler of all, and to Him the Angels who minister to each nation lead their followers.

Let us consider Melchisadek, the hierarch most beloved of God - not of vain gods, but a priest of the truly highest of Gods - for those wise in the things of God did not simply call Melchisadek the friend of God, but also priest, in order to show clearly to the wise that not only was he himself turned to Him who is truly God, but also, as hierarch, was the leader of others in the ascent to the true and only Godhead.

Let us also remind you in connection with your

knowledge of hierarchy that Pharaoh was shown through visions by the Angel who presided over the Egyptians, and the Prince of Babylon was shown by his own Angel, the watchful and overruling Power of Providence. And for those nations the servants of the true God were appointed as leaders, the interpretations of angelic visions having been revealed from God through Angels to holy men near to the Angels, like Daniel and Joseph.

For there is one Sovereign and Providence of all, and we must never suppose that God was leader of the Jews by chance, nor that certain Angels, either independently, or with equal rank, or in opposition to one another, ruled over the other nations; but this teaching must be received according to the following holy intention, not as meaning that God had shared the sovereignty of mankind with other Gods, or with Angels, and had been chosen by chance as ruler and leader of Israel, but as showing that although one all-powerful Providence of the Most High consigned the whole of mankind to the care of their own Angels for their preservation, yet the Israelites, almost alone of them all, turned to the knowledge and light of the true God.

Therefore the Word of God, when relating how Israel devoted himself to the worship of the true God, says, 'He became the Lord's portion'.

Moreover it shows that he too, equally with other nations, was given into the charge of one of the holy Angels, in order that he might know through him the one Principle of all things. For it says that Michael was the leader of the Jews, clearly showing that there is one Providence established superessentially above all the invisible and visible powers, and that all the Angels who preside over the different nations lift up to that Providence, as to their own Principle, as far as is in their power, those who willingly follow them.

CHAPTER X

Recapitulation and summary of the Angelic Hierarchies.

We have agreed that the most venerable Hierarchy of the Intelligences, which is close to God, is consecrated by His first and highest Ray, and uplifting itself directly to It, is purified, illuminated and perfected by the Light of the Godhead which is both more hidden and more revealed. It is more hidden because It is more intelligible, more simplifying, and more unitive, It is more revealed because It is the First Gift and the First Light, and more universal and more infused with the Godhead, as though transparent. And by this again the second in its own degree, and by the second the third, and by the third our hierarchy, according to the same law of the regular principle of order, in divine harmony and proportion, are hierarchically, led up to the super-primal Source and End of all good orders, according to that divinely established law.

Each Order is the interpreter and herald of those above it, the most venerable being the interpreter of God who inspires them, and the others in turn of those inspired by God. For that superessential harmony of all things has provided most completely for the holy regulation and the sure guidance of rational and intellectual beings by the establishment of the beautiful choirs of each Hierarchy; and we see that every Hierarchy possesses first, middle and last powers.

But to speak rightly, He also divided each rank in the same divine harmonies, and on this account the Scriptures say that the most divine Seraphim cry one to another, by which, as I think, it is clear that the first impart to the second their knowledge of divine things.

This may fittingly be added, that each Celestial and human intelligence contains in itself its own first, middle and last powers, which are manifested in a way analogous to the aforesaid ordination belonging to each of the Hierarchical illuminations; and accordingly each intelligence, as far as is right and attainable to it, participates in the most spotless purity, the most abundant light, and the most complete perfection. For nothing is self-perfect nor absolutely unindigent of perfection, save only That which is truly self-perfect and above all perfection.

CHAPTER XI

Why all the Celestial Hierarchies in common are called Celestial Powers.

Now that these things have been defined, the reason for applying the general name, Celestial Powers, to all the Angelic beings demands our consideration. For we cannot say of these, as we can of the Angels, that the Order of the holy Powers is the last of all; moreover, the higher Orders of beings, indeed, have part in the illuminations of the lowest, but the last by no means possess those of the first. And for this reason all the Divine Intelligences are called Celestial Powers, but never Seraphim or Thrones or Dominions; since the lowest do not share in the whole characteristics of the highest. For the Angels, and the Archangels above them, and the Principalities, and the ranks which are placed by theology after the Powers, are frequent1y called by us Celestial Powers, in common with all the other holy beings.

But we deny that in using the general name, Celestial Powers, for all we cause any confusion with regard to the characteristics of each Order. For all the Divine Celestial Intelligences are divided, according to the supermundane account of them, into three groups in respect of their essence, power and activity; and when we name all or some of them, loosely, Celestial Beings or Celestial Powers, we are referring to them indirectly in terms of that essence or power which each possesses.

But we must not assign the highest characteristics of the holy Powers (which we have already well distinguished) to all the natures wholly below them, for this would bring confusion into the clear and harmonious Order of Angels: for, as we have frequently rightly shown, the highest Orders possess in fullest measure the holy characteristics of the lower, but the lowest do not possess the pre-eminent unitive principles of those more venerable than themselves, because the First Radiance is imparted to them through the first Orders according to their capacity.

CHAPTER XII

Why the Hierarchs among men are called Angels.

Those who earnestly study the holy Scriptures sometimes ask, 'If the lowest ranks do not possess to the full the powers of those above them, why is our Hierarch called in the holy Word the Angel of the Omnipotent Lord?'

This, however, does not contradict what has been already defined. For we say that the lowest choirs do not possess the integral and pre-eminent power of the higher Orders, since they receive it partially, in the measure of their capacity, in accordance with the one harmonious and binding fellowship of all things.

For example, the choir of the holy Cherubim participates in higher wisdom and knowledge, whilst the Orders below them are themselves also partakers of wisdom and knowledge, but more partially, and in a lower degree proportioned to their capacity. For the universal participation in wisdom and knowledge is shared by all the Divine Intelligences, but the degree of participation, whether immediate and first, or second and inferior, is not common, but is determined for each by its own rank. This also may be rightly said of all the Divine Intelligences, that even as the first possess in the highest degree the holy characteristics of the Orders below them, so the lowest possess the powers of the higher, not in equal measure, but in a subordinate degree.

Therefore I do not think it unreasonable that the Scriptures should call our hierarchs Angels, since they participate according to their own power in the interpretative characteristic of the Angels, and uplift themselves, as far as is possible to man, into an assimilation to the Angels as revealers of truth.

You will find, moreover, that the Word of God not only calls these Celestial Beings above us Gods, but also gives this name to saintly men amongst us, and to those men who, in the highest degree, are lovers of God; although the First and Unmanifest God superessentially transcends all things, being enthroned above all, and therefore none of the beings or things which are can truly be said to be wholly like Him, save in so far as those intellectual and rational beings who are wholly turned towards union with Him, as far as is in their power, and who, uplifting themselves perpetually, as far as possible, to the Divine Radiance, in the imitation of God (if it be lawful so to speak) with all their powers, are thought worthy of the same divine name.

CHAPTER XIII

The reason why the prophet Isaiah is said to have been purified by the Seraphim.

Let us now deal to the best of our ability with the question why the Seraph is said to have been sent to one of the prophets. For someone may feel doubt or uncertainty as to why one of the beings of the highest rank is mentioned as cleansing the prophet, instead of one of the lower ranks of Angels.

Some, indeed, say that according to the description already given of the inter-relation of all the Intelligences, the passage does not refer to one of the first of the Intelligences nearest to God, as having come to purify the hierarch, but that one of those Angels who are our guardians was called by the same name as the Seraphim because of his sacred function of purifying the prophet, for the reason that the remission of sins and the regeneration of him who was purified to obedience to God was accomplished through fire. And they say also that the passage simply says one of the Seraphim, not of those established around God, but of the purifying powers which preside over us.

But another suggested to me a solution of the

problem by no means unlikely, for he said that the great Angel, whoever he may have been, who fashioned this vision for the purpose of instructing the prophet in divine matters, referred his own office of purification first to God, and after God to that first Hierarchy. And is not this statement true? For he who said this said that the Divine First Power goes forth visiting all things, and irresistibly penetrates all things, and yet is invisible to all, not only as superessentially transcending all things, but also because It transmits Its Providential Energies in a hidden way through all things. Moreover, It is revealed to all Intellectual Natures in due proportion, and bestows the radiance of Its Light upon the most exalted beings through whom, as leaders, It is imparted to the lower choirs in order according to their power of divine contemplation; or to speak in more simple terms, by way of illustration (for although natural things do not truly resemble God, who transcends all, yet they are more easily seen by us), the light of the sun passes readily through the first matter, for this is more transparent, and by means of this it displays more brightly its own brilliance; but when it falls upon some denser material it is shed forth again less brightly because the material which is illuminated is not adapted for the transmission of light, and after this it is little by little diminished until it hardly passes through at all. Similarly, the heat of fire imparts itself more readily to that which is more adapted to receive it, being yielding and conductive to its likeness; but upon substances of opposite nature which are resistant to it, either no effect at all or only a slight trace of the action of the fire appears; and what is more, when fire is applied to materials of opposite nature through the use of other substances receptive to it the fire first heats the material which is easily made hot, and through it, heats proportionately the water or other substance which does not so easily become hot.

Thus, according to the same law of the material order, the Fount of all order, visible and invisible, supernaturally shows forth the glory of Its own radiance in all-blessed outpourings of first manifestation to the highest beings, and through them those below them participate in the Divine Ray. For since these have the highest knowledge of God, and desire pre-eminently the Divine Goodness, they are thought worthy to become first workers, as far as can be attained, of the imitation of the Divine Power and Energy, and beneficently uplift those below them, as far as is in their power, to the same imitation by shedding abundantly upon them the splendour which has come upon themselves; while these, in turn, impart their light to lower choirs. And thus, throughout the whole Hierarchy, the higher impart that which they receive to the lower, and through the Divine Providence all are granted participation in the Divine Light in the measure of their receptivity. There is, therefore, one Source of Light for everything which is illuminated, namely, God, who by His Nature, truly and rightly, is the Essence of Light, and Cause of being and of vision. But it is ordained that in imitation of God each of the higher ranks of beings is the source in turn for the one which follows it; since the Divine Rays are passed through it to the other. Therefore the beings of all the Angelic ranks naturally consider the highest Order of the Celestial Intelligences as the source, after God, of all holy knowledge and imitation of God, because through them the Light of the Supreme God is imparted to all and to us. On this account they refer all holy works, in imitation of God, to God as the Ultimate Cause, but to the first Divine Intelligences as the first regulators and transmitters of Divine Energies.

Therefore the first Order of the holy Angels possesses above all others the characteristic of fire, and the abundant participation of Divine Wisdom, and the possession of the highest knowledge of the Divine Illuminations, and the characteristic of Thrones which symbolizes openness to the reception of God. The lower

Orders of the Celestial Beings participate also in these fiery, wise and God-receptive Powers, but in a lower degree, and as looking to those above them who, being thought worthy of the primary imitation of God, uplift them, as far as possible, into the likeness of God.

These holy characteristics in which the secondary natures are granted participation through the first, they ascribe to those very Intelligences, after God, as Hierarchs.

He who gave this explanation used to say that the vision was shown to the prophet by one of those holy and blessed Angels who preside over us, by whose enlightening guidance he was raised to that intellectual contemplation in which he beheld the most exalted Beings (to speak in symbols) established under God, with God and around God; and their super-princely Leader, ineffably uplifted above them all, established in the midst of the supremely exalted Powers.

The prophet, therefore, learned from these visions that, according to every superessential excellence, the divine One subsists in incomparable pre-eminence, excelling all visible and invisible powers, above and exempt from all; and that He bears no likeness even to those first-subsisting Beings; and moreover that He is the Principle and Cause of all being, and the Immutable Foundation of the abiding stability of things that are, from which the most exalted Powers have both their being and their well-being. Then he was instructed that the Divine Powers of the holy Scriptures, whose sacred name means 'The Fiery Ones', and of which we shall soon speak, as far as we can, led the upliftment of the fiery power towards the Divine Likeness.

When the holy prophet saw in the sacred vision of the sixfold wings the most high and absolute upliftment to the Divine in first, middle and last Intelligences, and beheld their many feet and many faces, and perceived that their eyes and their feet were covered by their wings, and that the middle wings were in ceaseless movement, he was guided to the intelligible knowledge of that which was seen through the revelation to him of the farreaching and far-seeing power of the most exalted Intelligences, and of their holy awe which they have in a supermundane manner in the bold and persistent and unending search into higher and deeper Mysteries, and the perfect harmony of their ceaseless activity in imitation of God, and their perpetual upward soaring to the heights. Moreover, he also learned that divine and most glorious song of praise; for the Angel who fashioned the vision gave, as far as possible, his own holy knowledge to the prophet. He also taught him that every participation in the Divine Light and Purity, as far as this may be attained, is a purification, even to the most pure. Having its source in the Most High God, it proceeds from the most exalted Causes in a superessential and hidden manner, traversing the whole of the Divine Intelligences, and yet it shows itself more clearly, and imparts itself more fully to the most exalted Powers around God.

But as to the secondary or last intellectual powers, or our own powers, in proportion as each is further from the Divine Likeness, so the Divine Ray enfolds Its most brilliant light within Its own ineffable and hidden Unity. Moreover, It illuminates the second Orders severally through the first, and in short, It comes forth originally into manifestation from the Unmanifest through the first Powers.

The prophet was taught by the Angel who was leading him to light that the divine purification, and all the other divine activities shining forth through the First Beings, are imparted to all the others in the measure of the fitness of each for the divine participations.

Wherefore he reasonably assigned to the Seraphim, after God, the characteristic of imparting purification by fire. And there is nothing unreasonable in the representation of the Seraph as purifying the prophet; for just as God

Himself, the cause of every purification, purifies all, or rather (to use a more familar illustration), just as our hierarch, when purifying or enlightening through his priests or ministers, may himself be said to purify and illuminate, because those orders which he has consecrated refer their sacred activities to him, so also the Angel who purifies the prophet refers his own purifying power and knowledge to God as its origin, but to the Seraph as the first- working Hierarch-as though saying with angelic reverence when instructing him who was being purified: 'There is an exempt Source and Essence and Creator and Cause of the purification effected in you by me, He who brings into being the First Beings, and holds them established round Himself, and preserves their changeless stability, and guides them towards the first participations in His own Providential Energies.' (For this, so he said who taught me, shows the mission of the Seraph.) 'But the Hierarch and Leader, after God, the first Order of the first Beings, by whom I was taught to perform the divine purifications, is that which purifies thee through me; and through it the Cause and Creator of all purification brought forth His Providential Energies to us from the hidden depths.'

Thus he taught me, and I in turn impart it to thee.

It is for thy intellectual and discriminating skill either to accept one of the two reasons given as a solution of the difficulty, and prefer that to the other as probable and reasonable and perhaps true, or to find from thyself something more akin to the real truth, or learn from another (God indeed giving the word, and Angels directing it), and then to reveal to us who love the Angels a clearer, and to me more welcome view, if such should be possible.

CHAPTER XIV

What the traditional number of the Angels signifies.

This also is worthy, I think, of intellectual consideration, that the scriptural tradition respecting the Angels gives their number as thousands of thousands and ten thousand times ten thousand, multiplying and repeating the very highest numbers we have, thus clearly showing that the Orders of the Celestial Beings are innumerable for us; so many are the blessed Hosts of the Supermundane Intelligences, wholly surpassing the feeble and limited range of our material numbers. And they are definitely known only by their own supermundane and celestial Intellect and the knowledge which is granted to them allbounteously by the All-knowing Mother-Wisdom of the Most High God, which is superessentially at once the substantiating Cause, the connecting Power, and the universal Consummation of all principles and things.

CHAPTER XV

What is the meaning of the formal semblances of the Angelic Powers? What of the fiery and the anthropomorphic? What is meant by their yes, nostrils, ears, mouths, touch, eyelids eyebrows their manhood, teeth, shoulders, arms, hands, heart, breasts, backs, feet and wings? What are the nakedness and the vesture, the shining raiment, the priestly insignia, the girdles? What are the rods, spears, battle-axes and measuring-lines? What are the winds and clouds? What is meant by their brass and electron? What are the choirs and the clapping of bands? What are the colours of the various jewels? What is the form of the lion, the ox, the eagle? What are the horses, and their various colours? What are the rivers, the chariots, the wheels? What is the so-called joy of the Angels?

Let us, if you are so disposed, now relax our mental vision from the effort of the contemplation of the sublimity of the Angels, and descend to the particularized, all-various expanse of the manifold diversity of forms in angelic images; and then return analytically from them, as from symbols, ascending again to the simplicity of the Celestial Intelligences. But first let me point out clearly to you that the explanations of the sacred likenesses represent the same Orders of Celestial Beings sometimes as leading, and again being led, and the last leading and the first being led, and the same ones, as has been said, having first, middle and last powers. But there is nothing unreasonable in the account, according to the following method of unfoldment.

If, indeed, we said that some are first governed by those above them, and afterwards govern those Orders, and that the highest, whilst leading the lowest ranks, are at the same time being led by those whom they are leading, the statement would be obviously absurd and wholly confused. But if we say that these holy Orders both lead and are led, but not the same ones, nor by the same ones, but that each is led by those above itself, and in turn leads those below it, we may reasonably say that the Scripture in its sacred symbolic presentation sometimes rightly and truly assigns the same powers to the first, middle and last ranks.

Wherefore the eager upward tending to those above them, and the constancy of their revolution around them, being guardians of their own powers, and their participation in the providential power of proceeding forth to those below them through their own inter-relations, will truly befit all the Celestial Beings, although some pre-eminently and universally, others in a partial and lower degree.

But we must begin to deal with the remaining part of our discourse, and must ask, in first explanation of the forms, why the Word of God prefers the sacred symbol of fire almost above all others. For you will find that it is used not only under the figure of fiery wheels, but also of living creatures of fire, and of men flashing like lightning who heap live coals of fire about the Heavenly Beings, and of irresistibly rushing rivers of flame. Also it says that the Thrones are of fire, and it shows from their name that the most exalted Seraphim themselves are burning with fire, assigning to them the qualities and forces of fire; and throughout, above and below, it gives the highest preference to the symbol of fire.

Therefore I think that this image of fire signifies the perfect conformity to God of the Celestial Intelligences For the holy prophets frequently liken that which is superessential and formless to fire which (if it may lawfully be said) possesses many resemblances as in visible things to the Divine Reality. For the sensible fire is in some manner in everything, and pervades all things without mingling with them, and is exempt from all things and, although wholly bright, yet lies essentially hidden and unknown when not in contact with any substance on which it can exert its own energy. It is irresistible and invisible, having absolute rule over all things, bringing under its own power all things in which it subsists. It has transforming power, and imparts itself in some measure to everything near it. It revives all things by its revivifying heat, and illuminates them all with its resplendent brightness. It is insuperable and pure, possessing separative power, but itself changeless, uplifting, penetrative, high, not held back by servile baseness, ever-moving, selfmoved, moving other things. It comprehends, but is incomprehensible, unindigent, mysteriously increasing itself and showing forth its majesty according to the nature of the substance receiving it, powerful, mighty, invisibly present to all things. When not thought of, it seems not to exist, but suddenly enkindles its light in the way proper to its nature by friction, as though seeking to do so, uncontrollably flying upwards without diminishing its all-blessed self-giving.

Thus many properties of fire may be found which symbolize through sensible images the Divine activities. Knowing this, those wise in the things of God have portrayed the Celestial Beings under the figure of fire, thus proclaiming their likeness to the Divine, and their imitation of Him in the measure of their power.

But they also invest them with the likeness of men because of the human powers of intellect and aspiration, the straight and erect form, the inherent power of guiding and governing; and because man, although least in sense-perception in comparison with the powers of irrational creatures, yet rules over them all through the pre-eminence of his intellect, the lordship of his rational knowledge, and the intrinsic freedom of his unconquerable soul.

Thus it is possible, I think, to find in the various parts of our bodies fitting symbols of the Celestial Powers by taking, for example, the power of sight as an image of their most transparent upliftment to the Divine Light, their single, free, unresisting reception of that Light, their responsiveness and pure receptivity without passion to the divine illuminations.

The human power of distinguishing odours signifies the power to receive the inconceivable and most fragrant divine influences, as far as is attainable, and the definite recognition and utter rejection of others not of this kind.

The power of the ears denotes participation in and conscious gnostic receptivity to divine inspiration. The power of taste represents an abundance of spiritual food and the reception of divine streams of nourishment.

The power of touch symbolizes the power of distinguishing that which is of advantage from that which is harmful. The eyelids and eyebrows represent the guarding of intellectual conceptions in divine contemplations. The images of youth and vigour denote their perpetual bloom and vigour of life. The teeth symbolize the distribution of the sustaining perfection supplied to them; for each Intellectual Order, receiving a unitive conception from the Divine, with Providential Power divides and multiplies it for the proportionate upliftment of the one below.

The shoulders, arms and hands signify the powers of activity and accomplishment. The heart is a symbol of that Divine Life which imparts its own life-giving power beneficently to those within its care. We may add that the chest, being placed over the heart, represents the indomitable power which guards its own life-giving dispensations. The back denotes that strength which holds together all the life-giving powers. The feet signify the power of motion, swiftness and skilfulness in the evermoving advance towards divine things. Wherefore the prophet described the feet of the Celestial Intelligences as being covered by their wings which symbolize a swift soaring to the heights, and the heavenly progression up the steep, and the exemption from everything earthly through the upward ascent. The lightness of the wings shows that they are altogether heavenly and unsullied and untrammelled in their upliftment on high. The naked and unshod feet symbolize their free, easy and unrestrained power, pure from all externality, and assimilated, as far as is attainable, to the Divine Simplicity.

But since that single and manifold Wisdom both clothes the naked and assigns to them implements to carry, let us unfold, as far as we can, these sacred garments and instruments of the Celestial Intelligences.

Their shining and fiery vestures symbolizes, I think, the Divine Likeness under the image of fire, and their own enlightening power, because they abide in Heaven, where Light is: and also it shows that they impart wholly intelligible Light, and are enlightened intellectually.

Their priestly garment symbolizes their authority as leaders to the mystical and divine contemplations, and the consecration of their whole life. The girdles denote their guardianship of their own generative power, and their state of unification, for they are wholly drawn together towards their essential unity surrounding it in a perfect circle with changeless sameness.

The rods are tokens of the authority of sovereignty and leadership and the true directing of all things. The spears and battle-axes represent the power of dividing incongruous things and the keen, vigorous and effectual power of discrimination. The measuring-lines and carpenters' tools are figures of the power of foundation and erection and perfection, and whatever else belongs to the providential guidance and upliftment of the lower orders. Sometimes, however, the implements assigned to the holy Angels symbolize the divine judgment upon ourselves; for some are figures of His corrective discipline of avenging justice, others of freedom from difficulties, or the perfection of disciplinary instruction, or the restoration to our first happiness, while others signify the addition of other gifts, great or small, sensible or intelligible; and no acute mind would have any difficulty at all in finding the correspondence between the visible symbols and the invisible realities.

The name winds given to the Angels denotes their swift operations, and their almost immediate impenetration of everything, and a transmitting power in all realms, reaching from the above to the below, and from the depths to the heights, and the power which uplifts the second natures to the height above them, and moves the first to a participative and providential upliftment of the lower.

But perhaps it may be said that the name winds, applied to the aerial spirit, signifies the Divine Likeness in the Celestial Beings. For the figure is a true image and type of Divine Energy (as is shown more fully in the Symbolical Theology in our fourfold explanation) corresponding to the moving and generative forces of Nature, and a swift and irresistible advance, and the mystery, unknown and unseen by us, of the motive principles and ends. For He says: 'Thou knowest not whence it cometh nor whither it goeth.' The Scriptures also depict them as a cloud, showing by this that these holy Intelligences are filled in a supermundane manner with the hidden Light, receiving that first revelation without undue glorying, and transmitting it with abundant brightness to the lower Orders as a secondary, proportionate illumination; and further, that they, possess generating, lifegiving, increasing and perfecting powers by reason of their intelligible outpourings, as of showers quickening the receptive womb of earth by fertilizing rains for life-giving travail. The Scriptures also liken the Celestial Beings to brass and electron, and many coloured jewels. Now electron, [an alloy of silver and gold] resembling both gold and silver, is like gold in its resistance to corruption unspent and undiminished, and its undimmed brightness; and is like silver in its shining and heavenly lustre. But the symbolism of brass (in line with the explanations already given) must resemble that of fire or gold. Again, of the many coloured varieties of stones, the white represents that which is luminous, and the red corresponds to fire, yellow to gold, and green to youth and vigour. Thus corresponding to each figure you will find a mystical interpretation which relates these symbolical images to the things above.

But now, since this has been sufficiently explained, I think, according to our ability, let us pass on to the sacred unfoldment of the symbolism which depicts the Celestial Intelligences in the likeness of beasts.

The form of a lion must be regarded as typifying their power of sovereignty, strength and indomitableness, and the ardent striving upward with all their powers to that most hidden, ineffable, mysterious Divine Unity and the covering of the intellectual foot-prints, (7) and the mystically modest concealment of the way leading to divine union through the Divine Illumination.

The figure of the ox signifies strength and vigour and the opening of the intellectual furrows to the reception of fertilizing showers; and the horns signify the guarding and unconquerable power.

The form of the eagle signifies royalty and high soaring and swiftness of flight and the eager seizing of that food which renews their strength, discretion, and ease of movement and skill, with strong intensity of vision which has the power to gaze unhindered, directly and unflinchingly upon the full and brilliant splendour of the brightness of the Divine Sun. The symbolism of horses represents obedience and tractability. The shining white horses denote clear truth and that which is perfectly assimilated to the Divine Light the dark, that which is hidden and secret; the red, fiery might and energy; the dappled black and white, that power which traverses all and connects the extremes, providentially and with perfecting power uniting the highest to the lowest and the lowest to the highest.

If we had not to bear in mind the length of our discourse, we might well describe the symbolic relations of the particular characteristics of animals already given, and all their bodily forms, with the powers of the Celestial Intelligences according to dissimilar similitudes: for example, their fury of anger represents an intellectual power of resistance of which anger is the last and faintest echo; their desire symbolizes the Divine Love; and in short, we might find in all the irrational tendencies and many parts of irrational creatures, figures of the immaterial conceptions and single powers of the Celestial Beings. This, however, is enough for the prudent, for one mystical interpretation will sufficiently serve as an example for the explanation of others of a similar kind.

We must now consider the representations of the Celestial Beings in connection with rivers and wheels and chariots. The rivers of flame denote those Divine Channels which fill them with super-abundant and eternally out-pouring streams and nourish their life-giving prolificness.

The chariots symbolize the conjoined fellowship of those of the same Order; the winged wheels, ever moving onward, never turning back or going aside, denote the power of their progressive energy on a straight and direct path in which all their intellectual revolutions are supermundanely guided upon that straight and unswerving course.

The figure of the spiritual wheels can also have another mystical meaning, for the prophet says that the name Gel, Gel is given to them, which in the Hebrew tongue means revolutions and revelations. For the divine fiery wheels truly revolve, by reason of their ceaseless movement, around the highest Good Itself, and they are granted revelations because to them the holy hidden Mysteries are made clear, and the earthly are lifted up, and the high illuminations are brought down and imparted to the lowest orders.

The last thing for us to explain is the joy attributed to the Celestial Orders. For they are utterly above and beyond our passionate pleasures. But they are said to rejoice with God over the finding of that which was lost, as well befits the Godlike mildness of their nature, and as befits their beneficent and boundless joy at the providential salvation of those who are turned to God, and that ineffable bliss in which holy men have often participated when the illuminations of God have divinely visited them.

Let this be a sufficient account of those sacred symbols which, although it falls far short of their full interpretation, will yet, I think, contribute to prevent us from lingering basely in the figures and forms themselves.

If you should point out that we have not mentioned in order all the Angelic powers, activities and images described in the scriptures, we should answer truly that we do not possess the supermundane knowledge of some, or rather that we have need of another to guide us to the light and instruct us; but others have been passed over for the sake of proportion, as being parallel to what has been given; and the hidden Mysteries which lie beyond our view we have honoured by silence.

The celestial hierarchy - Pseudo-Dionysius the Areopagite

Index

CHAPTER I 7

CHAPTER II 11

CHAPTER III 21

CHAPTER IV 25

CHAPTER V 31

CHAPTER VI 33

CHAPTER VII 35

CHAPTER VIII 43

CHAPTER IX 48

CHAPTER X 54

CHAPTER XI 56

CHAPTER XII 58

CHAPTER XIII 60

CHAPTER XIV 69

CHAPTER XV 70

Look for other classics of Christianity on:
LIMOVIA.NET

THANK YOU!

CPSIA information can be obtained
at www.ICGtesting.com
Printed in the USA
LVHW090743160221
679337LV00006B/114